From $6 an Hour to a Million Dollar Dream

The Process Isn't Easy, but Your Decisions Determine Your Outcome

D1300839

Cayman Kelly

Speak It To Book
www.speakittobook.com

From $6 an Hour to a Million Dollar Dream / Cayman Kelly
ISBN-13: 978-1-952602-07-8

Reading Cayman's book solidifies what I already knew: that he's one of the most positive, uplifting people in the radio business. His positivity and hustle are his superpowers, and if you read closely, he tries to share those powers with you. I'm honored to know you, Cayman, and I'm taking notes!

Wayne Brady
Actor, Comedian, Singer, Game Show Host

I've always been a fan of Cayman Kelly's work on the radio, and I'm glad to know him personally. What a treat to read his new book and find he's also a great writer! Drawing on his many years of experience, filled with anecdotes featuring a who's-who of stars, he's written an inspiring, entertaining, and practical book to help find your path to success.

Boney James
Saxophonist

Cayman Kelly has written a motivational workbook that anyone can use to not only stay inspired in the pursuit of their dreams, but also live in a space of accountability. This is the kind of book that can be returned to, anytime a new goal is being pursued.

Kenny Lattimore
Singer/Songwriter

Cayman is a wise man, and I love when honest men talk. You will always get an honest perspective on real life, helpful jewels that we *all* can apply! It's sincere, and it tries to show us all, based on his story, not only how to be successful but also how to make [success] last.

Shawn Stockman
Co-founding member of Boyz II Men

To my loving wife—I dedicate this book to you for being my greatest cheerleader and encouraging me to strive beyond mediocrity! You have helped to balance me out to become the man, the husband, the father, and the entrepreneur that I am.

To my three children, Katelyn, Tre, and Chase—I dedicate this book to you as well, in hopes that one day you will use my examples as a guide for your lives. I love you all!

Katelyn—you are an amazing young writer. You don't see it yet, but you are incredibly talented.
Tre—thank you for helping to design the cover of this book. You are a natural! Your future is promising.
Chase—you are so smart, and you inspire me every day by being so proud of your dad. By the way, thanks for contributing to this book by sharing your quote: "Live your dream and don't let anyone take it away from you."

And to my parents—it all started with you two. Thank you for the values that you have instilled in me.

CONTENTS

From Dream to Reality

What's your dream? Your passion? What's that *one thing* you want to do with your life?

Now think about *why* you want to pursue that particular dream. Maybe you have a talent you want to share with others. Maybe it's a vision you think could make a real difference in the world.

The question you may be asking yourself right now is: How do I turn my dream into something that can make a difference in my life and the lives of others?

I firmly believe that everyone has something unique to offer the world. That's right. I believe that *you* were born with the potential to do something great. How you use that potential (or don't) is completely up to you.

Why this book? Because everyone who decides to pursue a dream needs a starting point. One of my greatest passions is helping to provide aspiring entrepreneurs like you with the necessary tools to realize their dreams. In the pages ahead, I'll share tips I learned through building a career in radio and voice-over work, along with stories of people who have inspired or challenged me along the way. You'll find advice on how to evaluate ideas to determine which ones are action-worthy, why you need to create a plan for how to move ahead, and when to quit the day job. At the end of each chapter, a workbook section will take you deeper into the process of making your dreams a reality.

If you're looking to turn your talents and dreams into a viable business, there's one thing you need to know before you start: the grind is real. It's hard. It can be frightening at times and thrilling at others. But if you want to succeed, it's something you have to commit to seeing through, failures and all.

If you're ready to see your dreams through to success, then let's get started.

CHAPTER ONE

What's Your Gift?

I remember looking for work after graduating from college. I couldn't find anything I wanted to do. There seemed to be nothing that would really make me happy and also provide me with an income to take care of my necessities. So I began teaching at a school. It wasn't my ideal job, but it paid the bills.

At the same time, I was also hanging around a local radio station. I'd gotten my first experience working behind the scenes in high school (more on that later), and it stuck with me. Throughout my time in college, I kept contacts at the station where I had worked during my high school years.

After graduating from college with a degree in Mass Communications, I began the process of looking for a job. I was invited to a job fair by my friend Agnes, who was the receptionist at the radio station. She told me to meet them at the radio station the next morning. I arrived at the station earlier than the time she gave me, and I sat in the car, waiting to see where they were. No one was answering the phone, and I noticed that they had already left.

Instead of going home, I walked to the front door of the radio station and picked up the security phone in the front. I told them that I was there to see Albie Dee, the guy who had introduced me to radio in high school and who was on the air at the time. Albie accepted the call, and security buzzed the door for me to come in. In our conversation, I told Albie that I had graduated from college and was currently looking for a job. He replied, "I don't have a job to give you, but I could use some help on my show. It would be a great way to get your foot back in the door and allow people to see your work ethic."

I gladly accepted his offer to help him out! In the days that followed, I answered phones, took requests, and pulled the music and commercials for each hour of the show, among other things. Though I wasn't getting paid to be there, those hours were some of my happiest, and I knew that I somehow had to make a career in radio.

The thing that really motivated me to begin pursuing a career in the broadcast industry was the people who worked at the station. I appreciated how they took to me and how they interacted with me. I remember thinking, "Man, I really love this. I want to stay around this."

The Reason

There are similar stories from many artists I've talked to over the years who tried various things before they found their true passion. There's my good friend and brother Al B. Sure!, who wrote songs during high school and put them in a shoebox under his bed. He always had a love for music, but he also had a love for football and was a star quarterback for Mount Vernon High School. He found, however, that his passion for music was greater than his passion for football, which led him to turn down a scholarship from the University of Iowa so that he could focus more on his music interest.

Al B. Sure!'s decision to pursue his greater passion, despite what others around him might have thought about his choice, ended up being the best decision he could have made. He was selected by the great Quincy Jones as the winner of Sony Record's talent search contest. Those same songs that had been sitting underneath his bed in high school became platinum hits as well as his ticket to travel the world and perform in front of global audiences. Al B. Sure! went on to become one of the most prominent artists and producers in the New Jack Swing era.

I heard a similar story from an artist I met a few years ago while doing a live broadcast from the Essence Music Festival in New Orleans. I knew nothing about the artist, Mali Music, at the time, but when he spoke, I loved his spirit. I immediately could tell that he was destined for greatness.

As I dove deeper into Mali's story, I found out that he had two sisters and his mother was a single parent. When Mali's stepdad entered the picture, he was the first masculine image Mali had encountered, and that made him want to be a man. Mali was introduced to athletics, and he discovered that he had a natural skill set for playing football. He ended up getting a scholarship to an all-boys Catholic academy.

Mali told me, "In the South, playing football or basketball and getting a scholarship was a way out." He spoke about getting a private-school education and also learning the sport. He was ranked 21 in the state of Georgia, and he had a lot of scholarship offers. Everybody knew that football was his future, but he felt like he was just going through the motions to grow as a man. Deep down, his true passion was music. After all, he began acting as minister of music at his church at age eleven. He told his stepfather one day of his decision to pursue music, and his stepfather said, "You're going to do what? You're not about to be around here, sucking up my air."

Mali's stepfather might not have agreed with his decision to pursue music at the time, but he has since changed his mind. Mali put in the work and followed his passion to live out his true purpose in spite of what others thought. Now he's a Grammy-nominated artist who is loved by many.

Can your gifts, talents, and passions be used to impact your family, your city, even your world? Does that thought motivate you? If you're nodding your head yes, then you're on the right track. I believe that when we know *why* we're pursuing something, it helps us to focus our desires and motivates us with positivity. It also helps us to make a plan so we can put some steps into place and move toward our ultimate goal.

Chances are that you picked up this book because there's something you love doing, something that may or may not fit into the typical mold of what society deems normal in terms of building a career. In fact, your gifts and dreams may be pointing you in an entirely different direction, away from a traditional career path.

Young people of all generations have had desires to do things differently from what was expected of them. Often the older people in their lives are set in their life philosophies and do their best to talk the younger generation out of their "foolishness."

For the better part of a century now, the expectation has been to finish high school, go to college, and get a job right after graduating. The ideal life, according to that philosophy, is to hold on to that great-paying job until you retire. Once you retire, you can buy the fun things you couldn't justify purchasing when you were younger, and you can do the things you wanted to do but couldn't because your 9-to-5 job didn't allow you the flexibility to pursue those interests.

I'm of the opinion that you should work hard and play hard at the same time. Not everyone is going to agree with me on that, but I believe that it's important to pursue your dreams and develop your potential if you're going to live the fullest, most productive, and happiest life possible. After all, we don't really know how long we will live or how we are going to age. There's only one life to live, so make the best of it!

Your Gift Has a Purpose

When my friends are going through low points in their careers or they feel like they're in a dead end and they want to give up, I tell them, "I don't believe God blessed you with a gift just for you to keep it to yourself, and it's really not your gift to give up on. You have an obligation to be a blessing with what you have been blessed with."

In my personal scenario, I had a detailed plan of how to get where I was going. It just so happened that some of the things I needed to happen in order for me to reach my goal actually fell into place. I didn't really know what I was doing at first. I just had the focus and drive to pursue my dream of working in radio and, ultimately, to make a career out of doing voice-over work. There were so many obstacles, and I could easily have turned around and found something else to do. But I stayed focused on the prize, and it made all the difference.

You were born with gifts, and it's up to you to nurture them. Some people recognize their gifts and spend their entire lives cultivating and developing them. Others stumble across their gifts later in life and wonder why they didn't recognize them sooner. Then there are those who never recognize or use their gifts at all. They go through life feeling unhappy and unfulfilled. They may even blame others for their unhappiness. You don't want to be that person.

No matter your age, it's not too late for you to put your gifts to work. But if you decide to go down this path, you have to realize that it's going to require time and effort— a lot of it. You can't expect to wake up one day and decide, "Hey, I've got this gift, and I'm going to use it to change the world," and then expect the world immediately to recognize who you are and what you're doing. First, you've got to put in the effort.

I like to tell the artists who are just starting their careers, "You know, a lot of people won't know about you unless you put yourself out there."

Author Jeff Goins shared similar advice when he wrote, "There is no better way to improve than to put your work out there—sharing it for the whole world to see—no other way to get discovered than to risk rejection. You have to practice in public."[1]

You can have the greatest gift in the world, but unless you share it, it doesn't really exist. A dream or a thought has no substance in itself. It requires you to put some feet on it for it to take its final form. In the same way, a goal is not realized when you do nothing. It takes practice, dedication, and forward movement in order to reach it. A thought is only a thought unless it's placed into action. You have to chase your dream and use your gift to gain satisfaction.

There's a real difference between the job you begrudgingly show up for every day and a career that is fueled by passion and fully utilizes your gifts. You may not like the job you have, but can you use it to move you toward the career you want?

Consider if there are any opportunities you can use to get your feet wet in a field you are passionate about. It could be through volunteering or applying for an internship. Whatever way you get started, finding a way to gain first-hand experience won't just help you to take the first steps in realizing your dream; it will also help you to start to form a network that may open up different experiences you might not previously have considered exploring.

My Dream

I wasn't what you'd call a star student growing up. It

wasn't that I didn't like learning; academics just didn't hold my focus. But *creating*, now that was another story. Even from an early age, I loved to write and draw. My mother was a piano player, and she wanted me to learn the piano. I could have learned if I'd cared to take the time, but I didn't want to play the piano.

I started out wanting to play the drums. I took lessons, but when it got hard, I quit. Then I thought that I *really* wanted to play the saxophone, but my dad started to see a pattern in the way I didn't stick to things I started. Since he already owned a guitar, he offered to pay for guitar lessons. I didn't know it then, but those childhood interests all stemmed from a gift I'd been born with. Once I learned to recognize it, that gift would set the tone and the trajectory of my life's journey.

Eventually, my love for music motivated me to learn how to play the piano on my own, which eventually blossomed into creating my own music. I put together a group with my childhood friend Corey, who had an amazing talent with words. We wrote songs together and sang those songs in our church.

Throughout this time, we had the opportunity to perform on a local cable channel and on numerous stages in and out of town. Our biggest highlight was the time Corey called the radio station and rapped about a contest they were doing. That call led to us being invited to the radio station for a visit. From that visit, we formed relationships with the radio station, and the door opened for us to do raps about "the happenings" once a week. Eventually we created an intro for the afternoon-drive show host, Albie Dee, that played every day.

Through all of these experiences, I fell in love with radio and developed a strong desire to be on the air. One step led to another until I discovered that it wasn't just a fun part of my younger days; it was my dream.

Pursue Your Potential

Myles Munroe, one of my favorite authors, wrote:[2]

> The wealthiest place in the world is not the gold mines of South America or the oil fields of Iraq or Iran. They are not the diamond mines of South Africa or the banks of the world. The wealthiest place on the planet is just down the road. It is the cemetery. There lie buried companies that were never started, inventions that were never made, bestselling books that were never written, and masterpieces that were never painted. In the cemetery is buried the greatest treasure of untapped potential.

Just think. Buried in the cemetery are people who had vast ideas and dreams, but they never took the actions necessary to give the world what they had to offer. Maybe there was never any motivation behind the thought, or perhaps they never developed the drive even to try turning the thought into something tangible. Maybe they did try, but they got discouraged when it didn't work out the way they envisioned, and they didn't try again.

The greatest failure doesn't come from pursuing your potential and potentially falling short. It comes from not pursuing your potential at all. Success requires drive, and you need to be able to push through those obstacles and those bad times in your life. Only you can determine how far you want to take that thought, that vision, that passion.

If you're not motivated and you don't put anything into action, then you're not growing, which means that you're stagnant. If you're stagnant, what's your purpose? What is your quality of life? What are you offering to the world?

Martin Luther King Jr. said, "If a man hasn't discovered something he will die for, he isn't fit to live."[3] In other words, everyone is here for a purpose. Everyone has a role to play. Once you find your purpose, you need to act on that purpose for the betterment of the world and for society.

The statement reminds me of a movie called *187* that sums up this concept perfectly.[4] Samuel L. Jackson plays a schoolteacher, Garfield, in a challenging school. In the film, some students try to kill his character, but they merely injure him by stabbing him. Garfield struggles to remain a good teacher, but he can't summon the strength to do it. This speaks to how our outside influences can put a damper on our dreams.

Later in the movie, Garfield's main threat, Cesar, breaks into his home, and they play Russian roulette with each other. Garfield exclaims, "You can't kill me. You know why? Because I'm already dead. I was a teacher. … I wanted to help you, and you took that from me."

Somebody snatched his purpose from him. Since he had lost his purpose, he referred to himself as already dead. What's the ultimate cost of not finding and using your gifts? In a word, death.

Learn to Put Your Gifts to Use

Fortunately for you, there are many unique ways to find your purpose and put it to use. If you're sitting there wondering, "How do I do that?" all you've got to do is look around.

Earlier in the chapter, I mentioned that sometimes you have to get your foot in the door by volunteering or finding an internship. Take opportunities, no matter how small, that can propel you toward your goal or help you to narrow your search for what you want to do. With the advent of social media, you can find others who are doing something similar and see what steps they're taking to grow their gifts.

Another thing you can do is read. When you read articles about successful people or listen to their interviews, one of the things you'll often find is that they're readers. They read magazines, biographies, and books by other people in their field. When I was starting out in the radio biz, I was reading books about successful people who inspired me. I remember reading about how Colonel Sanders had a successful local restaurant that he ended up selling when customer traffic was reduced by highway reconstruction. But he didn't give up because of a fail. Instead he drove around with his chicken recipe, looking for likely restaurants to franchise it. Traveling to solicit so many restaurants, sometimes he even had to sleep in the back of his car. His determination and persistence would lead to all of the later successes of Kentucky Fried Chicken, now known as KFC.[5]

If there's one thing I've learned from stories like

Colonel Sanders's, it's that developing a stick-to-it attitude sets you up for success later on. The more I read stories about the people who were brave enough to pursue their dreams, the more I'm inspired to pursue my own.

So there you have it. You have gifts, and you get to decide how you will use them. What are you going to do next?

Chapter One Questions

Question: What is the gift, talent, or passion that motivates you toward action? What brings you joy even if you aren't being paid to do it? In what ways is this dream countercultural? In what ways could it impact culture?

_____

_____

_____

_____

_____

_____

_____

_____

_____

_____

Question: What are some ways you will have to put yourself out there in order to be successful at your dream? What internal hesitations or external forces are holding you back from doing so?

_____

_____

_____

_____

_____

_____

_____

_____

_____

_____

Question: The greatest failure comes from not pursuing your potential at all. Think of an example of a person you know or know about who did not pursue his or her potential or take action on his or her God-given gifts. What can you learn from this person's story?

_____

_____

_____

_____

_____

_____

_____

_____

_____

_____

_____

Action: Make a list of steps you can take today to pursue your passion. These may include ways and places to volunteer, books to read, and people with whom to network. Now choose one of these steps to begin working on this week.

Chapter One Notes

_____

_____

_____

_____

_____

_____

_____

_____

_____

_____

_____

_____

_____

_____

_____

_____

_____

_____

_____

_____

_____

_____

CHAPTER TWO

Developing Your Gift

When I was in high school, my friend Corey used to write songs, and I'd put the music behind them. We had a song called "Action." The song was about the ills happening in society and how we can't just sit around and wait for them to correct themselves. Action needs to be taken if things are ever going to change.

I'll always remember one of the lines from that song: "A thought is a thought unless placed into action." As I really began pursuing my passion for radio and voice-over work, I took that quote and applied it to my life. To this day, when I fall into a slump, get discouraged, or feel like I failed at something, remembering that line gives me the motivation to keep going. It reminds me that my desires and gifts aren't going to do anything for themselves. I have to put in the *action* to make things *happen*.

Find Your Passion

In the last chapter, I asked if the thing you're passionate about could make a difference in the lives of the people around you. Part of developing your gifts is learning how to distinguish good ideas you can really build upon from fleeting thoughts that are based on emotion and will pass quickly. When an idea enters your mind, ask yourself, "How is this idea going to impact other people, my family, and myself in positive ways?" Then ask yourself if it's something that you're willing to commit years to developing fully.

Working through those initial questions really kicks off the motivation for pursuing your dream. That's when you start to find your passion. In the process, it's important to remember that ideas don't become careers or businesses on their own.

Take my start in radio, for example. Initially I wasn't getting paid to be there, but I loved it so much that working for free didn't bother me. This spoke to my level of commitment and what I was willing to put up with to obtain my goal of having a career in radio. Once other decision-makers started to recognize me around the radio station, I did a lot of things unrelated to radio, such as moving chairs, putting things in closets, and organizing records in the music library.

But the grunt work didn't go unnoticed, and it eventually turned into an opportunity to run the boards for live, on-location broadcasts. After that, I worked in promotions, which allowed me to be heard on the air by those calling in from various locations in the city. Next thing I knew, I had reached the ultimate goal of being on the air and doing a real, full show. You just don't know when your breakthrough will come. That's why it's so important to take small steps, make use of every opportunity, and keep putting in the work at all times.

If you're not actively moving forward in your dream and developing your gifts, you can't expect to begin making money or building a name for yourself. You have to be willing to make a change. If you're going to put in the effort, you also have to be willing to commit to following through, no matter how tough things might get.

Follow Through

If you want to be successful, it's not enough merely to start. You need to look for new ways to grow, and when you spot the areas where you need growth, you have to follow through.

My first paid job at the radio station was working in promotions. I had previously learned to operate the board for live broadcasts, and one day the overnight personality got sick, which gave me my first opportunity to get on the air as a personality.

I did the overnight shift for a few months as a part-time employee without a contract, making about $6 per hour at a top-ten-market radio station. This was a paltry amount compared to others in the field. I was under the impression that if I did a good job, the program director (PD) would come to me and offer me the job as a full-time position with the pay of a typical radio personality and benefits.

A few months down the road, I met up with my PD for

a review, and he told me, "You are a great guy. Everyone loves you, but your follow-up is weak."

I asked, "What do you mean by that?"

He said, "You have been doing the overnight air position for a few months now, and never once have you brought me a pitch that you want this as a full-time job."

I was surprised by his comments. I thought that he would approach me with an offer if I showed my potential, but that wasn't how things worked around there.

"If you don't take the initiative to speak up for yourself," my PD said, "we will roll right over you."

This was one of the first moments that made me realize I had to take action and responsibility for myself. That's what made me focus on my ultimate goal and start to think, "If I don't put my best foot forward and become assertive, no one is ever going to recognize the talent I have." I discovered that I might get chances when things happened to fall into place, but if I wanted to move forward, I had to put in the effort, learn to speak up on my own behalf, and put myself out there.

Maybe you're in a similar place. You've got your foot in the door, but you're not gaining any noticeable traction. Take a look around you. What are other people who are having success in your field doing to get ahead? Are they signing up for seminars? Taking lessons? Finding mentors? They're doing something, and it isn't standing still, waiting for things to change on their own.

Take my friend Bobby Brown, for instance, who grew up in the Orchard Park Projects in the Roxbury section of Boston. He said that he always had dreams to be a star. He decided to put some action behind those dreams, and he pulled some of his neighborhood friends together to form the group New Edition. I have talked to several of the members about their early beginnings, and they all credit Bobby for being the one who formed the group and kept it together. They would always rehearse at his house. All of that effort finally paid off when they entered a talent competition and ended up receiving a recording contract, which would later lead them to become pop sensations in the early 1980s.

When the group later voted Bobby out, he easily could have given up, but instead he secured a record deal as a solo artist and released his debut album, *King of the Stage*. That album produced a number-one hit song, but the album wasn't a commercial success. Bobby told me that he laid low for a little while and took notice of the producers and songwriters who were hot in the industry. Then he started reaching out to them to put his next album together. Almost two years later, Bobby released the biggest album of his career, *Don't Be Cruel*, from which he had five Top 10 hits, including "My Prerogative," a song that he wrote himself and which became a Number 1 hit.

Bobby sold more than 12 million albums worldwide, won his first Grammy and two American Music Awards, and more. Despite all of the tragedies, losses, and addiction that he has experienced throughout his life, he has been a blessing to many by being transparent and a great illustration of how to continue moving forward.

Taking the Ultimate Risk

When you make the decision to pursue your passion

and develop your gifts to their full potential, there will come a day when you'll have to make the choice to take the ultimate risk. This is the day when you'll go from just dreaming about an idea to sharing it with the world. In order to get to that point, you must have a plan in place because you'll still have responsibilities and obligations. This is especially true if you're married or you have a family depending on you.

Right before I got married, I took my first leap into a position at a third-party channel that provided content for the new technology of the time, XM Satellite Radio. I was making the most money I had ever made in my radio career. While I was on this job, I had the opportunity to meet many amazing people, which resulted in connections that led me to an on-the-side opportunity. I was presented with the opportunity to do something I had always dreamed of doing: voice-overs.

Unfortunately, the job providing content for XM Satellite Radio only lasted about a year, and I was left scrambling, trying to figure out what to do next. During that limbo period, I continued to do voice-overs on the side. I did not recognize it as real work, but I was getting paid to use my voice for commercials and promos for TV. This very thing kept my bills paid on time.

While I was still trying to figure out where I was going, my wife and I welcomed our first child. I started another job working directly at the headquarters of XM Satellite Radio the week after my daughter was born. I was hired to program a specific channel as well as to be on the air. In the evening, I was still working at another radio station. When I got home, I had voice work to do, as well as helping my wife with the newborn.

Over the next few years, we welcomed another child to the family. Our finances and jobs were pretty stable at that point. It was challenging trying to balance a work life and a family life, but we rose to the occasion.

Soon after, I started experiencing turbulence on the job front when I got word of a merger happening at XM Radio. This merger caused a lot of uncertainty and fear. During the process of the merger, a lot of people I had worked with for a number of years were let go. It hurt me so much to see this happening. I even cried over it! Fortunately, I survived the merger and was able to keep working. Thank God!

Back on the family front, we added a third child to the mix. Now it was really a juggling act! My wife had her career, I had mine, and we had the kids to take care of. Since I had the most flexibility with my job, I did the three different morning drop-offs with the kids and then fought traffic to get to my job in the city. At the end of the day, I drove thirty to forty miles to pick up all three kids, got them home, and made sure that everyone was fed and bathed. This became a normal routine, but it didn't change the fact that it was a balancing act. I was exhausted at the end of each day. Sometimes I would have to stay up late in order to complete work I hadn't finished during the course of the day.

Things eventually started to show a bit of promise when I got a call from an agency that was looking to represent me for my voice-over work. I was the voice of Black Entertainment Television (BET) and had been for about six years when I received the call from the agency.

I decided that I would sign with them to try to increase my voice-over imprint.

I auditioned a lot, but I wasn't landing any new work. It was a frustrating process. However, at my full-time job with XM Radio, I met a guy named Bryan Apple. Bryan did imaging production, which requires a lot of creativity. His job was to put together an audio piece that was sonically appealing and catchy through the use of music, voice, created sound effects, etc. Since I had a lot of ideas and I was good at writing and finding elements, he and I started to collaborate on some production pieces. We worked well together, and we turned out some award-winning stuff at work.

Meeting Bryan would prove to be a valuable friendship. He had worked in a lot of different radio markets and knew a lot of people I didn't. Through him, I was able to increase my network.

One connection he made for me eventually changed my life. He introduced me to a guy named Kwazi. Kwazi and Bryan did the same job when they worked in L.A. together, but now Kwazi was in New York at POWER 1051. The station was in the process of changing its personality to compete with other stations. They were looking for a new voice for the station, so Bryan said, "Let's put together a demo and send it to Kwazi and see what happens."

Kwazi liked our demo and gave it to his boss, Cadillac Jack, to see if he would consider using me. Of course, there was some apprehension because I had never done this type of voice-over before. Long story short, he ended up giving me a try. I entered a voice-over world I had never considered: radio imaging voice.

This got the ball rolling, and more radio stations across the country began expressing interest in using me as their voice. From the agency auditions, I started to book jobs, including some for TV Land. This voice-over thing looked like it was starting to take shape.

That's when my wife started asking, "How long are you going to continue working your full-time job on top of doing voice-over work? How many more stations do you need to voice before you'd consider leaving?"

I shot out a random number and said, "If I get six radio stations to voice, I will leave my full-time job!"

I thought that it would be a long time before I got six stations, but it wasn't long at all! I considered going back on my promise because I still enjoyed being on the radio as a personality, too.

I continued doing both jobs, but my wife kept bringing up the possibility of me leaving my full-time job. She expressed how much more comfortable our lifestyle would be if I didn't have to rush in and out of the city every day. My commute would consist of walking down the steps, and we would no longer need to find somebody to watch the kids on their days out of school. All of those things sounded good, but I was still torn.

Then one day, out of the blue, my wife said, "I really think God wants to bless you in your voice-over work, but you won't let go of what's holding you back. He can't bless you with what He has in store for you if you keep holding on." I heard her, but I didn't want to listen.

Then I really started to process everything she had been telling me, and I challenged myself to exercise the faith I claimed to have. I prayed and read a lot about other entrepreneurs and the struggles they faced. I felt more and more comfortable about actually leaving my full-time job.

I told my wife, "You know what? December is going to be my last month. I'm going to leave my job at the end of this year."

As December approached, my heart raced with anxiety. Every time I thought I had the nerve to tell my boss that I was leaving, either he was not in his office or I couldn't gather the strength to say it. I finally saw him in his office and went to tell him of my decision. We had the conversation, and I felt a huge sense of relief. I was glad to have the conversation over with, but I was still scared because I didn't know what the future looked like.

Leaving my job wasn't easy. I'd been doing it for years, and it was comfortable. It was a good job, and though I might not have enjoyed everything about it, that's life. I knew that one of the most difficult parts about leaving would be not seeing the people I worked with every day. They had become like family to me.

However, there was a big surprise in store for me when I exercised my faith. I was actually able to keep my radio show with them and eliminate all the other aspects of the job, such as scheduling music, meetings, and the day-to-day tasks that went into running the radio channel. Since I already had a studio in my house where I conducted my voice-overs, I was allowed to utilize my own studio to do my radio show from home as well.

It ended up being the best of both worlds. I was able to have my own show, to be the voice for several other stations, and to do it all from the comfort of my own home.

I took a leap of faith, and I was not disappointed.

Today may not be the day you take the ultimate risk, but you need to be at least working toward it. If you don't already have one in place, now is the time to start creating a timeline for when you plan to say, "This is it. I may be scared, but it's time."

Think about the things you need to do in order for you to step out of your day job and into your passion career. What can you be doing during your evenings or on the weekends to set things in motion? Evaluate what needs to be done and *do it*.

If you want to live your most successful, satisfied life, you have to be willing to experience the discomfort that comes with risk. Prepare to take that leap of faith looming before you and watch your wildest dreams come true.

WORKBOOK

Chapter Two Questions

Question: A thought is only a thought unless it's put into action. What great ideas or important thoughts are you passionate about? How can each of them translate into an action?

_____

_____

_____

_____

_____

_____

_____

_____

_____

_____

Question: In what ways would utilizing your gifts benefit you, your family, and others? How do you know whether this is something in which you want to invest your life or just an interesting but passing idea?

_____

_____

_____

_____

_____

_____

_____

_____

_____

_____

Question: Consider individuals who are successful in your field. What have they done and what are they continuing to do to achieve their dreams? How can you grow by following their example?

_____

_____

_____

_____

_____

_____

_____

_____

_____

_____

_____

_____

Action: Write out a plan of what needs to happen before you step out of your day job to pursue your dream career. What factors need to be in place in your finances, family, training, and experience before you are ready for this step? It may be helpful to talk through your plan with your spouse and/or a mentor to make sure that you have a balance of security and calculated risk.

Chapter Two Notes

_____

_____

_____

_____

_____

_____

_____

_____

_____

_____

_____

_____

_____

_____

_____

_____

_____

_____

_____

_____

CHAPTER THREE

Motivators and Cheerleaders

When you look at the lives of successful people, you're going to find that they've surrounded themselves with like-minded people and a strong network of supporters and cheerleaders. These individuals have learned that if you're going to build a dream, you're going to need a team. You need people in your life who recognize your potential and give you a nudge or a push when you need an extra dose of motivation.

This is especially true when we experience moments of anxiety or panic. In my experience, I believe that support groups are one of the best methods of coping. Take Alcoholics Anonymous (AA), for example. AA is a group of people who have gone through similar things, and they know that they can safely talk with each other about their struggles. It acts as a support group to help people overcome their struggles and accomplish their goals.

Successful people don't try to carry heavy burdens on their own or attempt to do all the work themselves.

Successful people look for and accept help from others, which helps them to direct their energy toward a purpose and a goal rather than spinning their wheels when they're feeling worn out or stuck.

Who Are Your Cheerleaders?

Take a look around you. Who are the supportive people in your life? I count myself fortunate that I have supportive parents whom I can talk to and lean into. They were my initial source of motivation. When I fell, they built me back up. Because I learned that I could trust them when I was young, our relationship moved beyond the parent-child relationship when I got older. They became trusted friends, and I go to them about things I didn't feel comfortable talking to them about when I was a child.

And then there's my wife. I knew what potential lay inside of me, but it was my wife who drew it out into the open. It was my wife who pushed me to enroll in voice-over classes. She wrote the check and said, "This is something you gotta do now." In class, I found a mentor and a network that God was building in my life to open doors to opportunities that otherwise would have been closed to me.

I am so grateful that my wife supported my dream. She is wise, and I learn from her example, both professionally and personally. She is bold in the way she handles work obligations and responds to situations in her career that aren't conducive to her ideal lifestyle or her family's well-being. She makes necessary changes and doesn't just stick it out for the sake of the job and money. If a situation isn't right, she removes herself from it. To watch her in action is nothing short of inspiring.

My wife isn't afraid to speak the hard truths I need to hear. Before I took the leap to pursue my dream, my wife saw how unhappy I was in trying to make an unfulfilling job work. She relentlessly encouraged me to make the final transition and fully pursue the path I found fulfilling.

She is my greatest cheerleader and a testament to everyone's need for cheerleaders. They shore you up and let you know when you're holding on to something that is preventing you from moving forward in building your dream. Maybe it's a job, a bad relationship, the fear of failing, or even the fear of succeeding. Leaning into your long-term, healthy relationships can be invaluable in providing you with the support and encouragement needed to create a successful future. These connections, be they friends or family, can help you to determine areas where you're sabotaging yourself and give you the extra push you need to go after your dreams.

Beyond the Home

You may be wondering, "What if I don't have a supportive family? Who am I supposed to turn to?"

I get that.

Whether your family is supportive or not, it's important to build up a support network outside of your home. It could be a former teacher, a coach, or someone you met and connected with at a conference or networking event. You may meet cheerleaders in the last place you'd expect to find them.

Years ago, I booked a narration gig and set up some time to use the equipment at Ott House Studios. I was introduced to the owner, Cheryl, when I went in to record my project, and she and I hit it off right away.

She told me, "I love your voice. Make sure I get your number before you leave here." Then she said, "Just give it to me now, so we don't go through the session and forget about it later."

I gave her my contact info and didn't think much more of it until about a week later when I received an email from a lady at TV One saying that Cheryl had recommended me to them. They were looking for someone to do the voice promos for one of their biggest shows, and based on Cheryl's suggestion, they wanted to book me for recording the next day.

My point? A cheerleader can come in the form of someone you just met who recognizes your talent and plugs you into his or her network. More than cheerleaders, these people are influencers, and they're an invaluable part of your growing network.

Why You Need a Network

I'm a firm believer that people can't do things on their own. We are created to work in unison with one another. There are people, like my friend Cheryl, who can see your gifts. There are also people who will pull you back from the edge on those days when you're asking, "Did I really choose the right thing to do with my life?"

This is why networking is important. As you build relationships with other people, new opportunities will appear because someone in your network will hear about something he or she thinks you'd be perfect for. You, in turn, may hear of something that will benefit someone you know.

You never know when those connections you made long ago will come back into your present, just when you need a breakthrough. As I mentioned earlier, when I was looking for a job after college, I had a run-in with Albie Dee. We first met back when I was fifteen and writing music with my friend Corey. Albie was working at a radio station where I wanted to get a job, and we got to talking about my situation. Albie told me, "I don't have a job to give you, but you can help me out on my show. This may lead to other avenues, and it might be a way to get your foot in the door."

I got my first paid job at that radio station based on my dedication and the work I put in to establish a rapport with the people there. I learned and did a lot at that station, including running the boards, working in promotions, and eventually doing an on-air shift. However, all good things must come to an end.

After that job, I was hired by the competing radio station. The people I met there and beyond helped me in my future endeavors. I met my first attorney through that job. My attorney helped me with my first contract and later helped me to find another job at BET. From there, I met the people who worked the TV side. That, in turn, opened doors for me to do what I had wanted to do for years and years: voice-overs.

When it comes down to business, having the support of friends and family makes a difference, but I learned early on that having a network beyond family can open doors. When I grew out of my timidity, I saw things come together, and I recognized the importance of networking. When you've got a solid team behind you, there's no telling how far you'll go.

As I think about the importance of a network, there are many conversations that come to mind as examples of how vital these relationships are. Years ago, I got a phone call asking me to come into the president of XM's office because someone wanted to meet me. When I arrived, I saw Ludacris sitting on the floor. They had just signed him to do a show for XM Satellite Radio. He got up off the floor, gave me a hug, and told me how much he enjoyed listening to me on the air. He even went as far as to tell me things that I said on the radio. Then he said, "I promise you, if you had ever sent me a shout out, I would have peed on myself like a little girl!"

I said, "Man, what? You used to do radio, too! What makes me so special?"

I told him that I was a fan of all the things he was doing. As we stood in that office and had a conversation, I told him that I was familiar with him for doing the radio intro for Coco Brother, who used to come on the radio before my show. I asked him about his transition into artistry from radio and then on to acting. As he answered my questions, he talked about the importance of surrounding yourself with a team that has your best interest at heart.

He still has the same team today that he had during our meeting years ago. They've never had a contract with one another, they've never had any money issues, and they've been able to build an empire, including a record label, restaurants, and executive production of TV and film. That just goes to show you how important it is to build a network of people you can trust and rely on.

Your dreams won't become reality if you walk alone. You need someone to motivate you when you fall into slumps and feel like you don't have the strength to go any further. You need someone to recognize your gifts and to take a chance on you. There's always a starting point for everything you do in life, and those starting points can turn into a robust network of opportunity.

What opportunities are in front of you? Walk into them and watch how those connections fit together and help you to unlock your full potential.

WORKBOOK

Chapter Three Questions

Question: Do you readily accept help from others, or do you feel that you have to or should do everything on your own? What are some possible motivations behind this sort of independent or isolationist mindset? Why is it dangerous, and how can you become more comfortable with asking for and accepting others' help?

_____

_____

_____

_____

_____

_____

_____

_____

_____

_____

Question: Who are your cheerleaders, the people who believe in you and encourage you? What have you learned from them, and how have they helped you through difficulties, hesitation, fears, and obstacles?

_____

_____

_____

_____

_____

_____

_____

_____

_____

_____

Question: Beyond close family or friends, who is or could be part of your network? Where is your network strong, and where does it need to grow? Identify three people to reach out to and build into your network of positive influencers. Identify people in your network whom you need to keep in touch with more regularly or follow up with regarding an idea or offer of help.

_____

_____

_____

_____

_____

_____

_____

_____

_____

_____

_____

Action: Take time to thank someone who has been a cheerleader in your life. A note or message can let this person know what an influence he or she has had in your life and how much you appreciate it.

How can you be a cheerleader for someone just starting in your field or industry? How can you be a part of his or her network? Look for an opportunity this week to come alongside someone else, see his or her potential, and offer encouragement.

Chapter Three Notes

CHAPTER FOUR

Haters and Naysayers

Let's face it. Nobody likes a hater. You know the type: the individual who goes out of his or her way to bring you down or sabotage your work. Haters are those people who constantly challenge you, contradict you, and serve as reminders of things you didn't follow through on. They build themselves up at your expense.

But did you know that you can take their negativity and turn it into an advantage? Haters are a pain to deal with, but they're necessary for your journey. Believe it or not, if you only have people who agree with you and tell you how great you are, then you miss out on potential opportunities for growth. When you learn how to deal with the haters correctly, they can be motivators.

I ran into my first hater at a radio station where I volunteered right out of college. He was the intern coordinator, and for some reason, I always felt like he didn't care much for me. He would look at me a certain way, and I noticed that he would whisper to other people when I was around. One day, I got a call asking why I wasn't at work. I later discovered that the intern director had lied and told them that I was on the schedule, even though he'd told me that I was off for the day.

I never understood why this guy had it out for me. As far as I knew, I never did anything to him to warrant his animosity. Then I overheard him tell somebody, "Yeah, I'm watching that guy right there. He will mess around and take my job one day." He said it like it was a joke, but most of the time, there is truth inside a joke.

There are a number of ways I could have handled that situation badly, but I chose to do my best and to prove that I was a valuable staff member. And I kept my ears open. When I found out that he was encouraging another intern to apply for a position I hadn't been told about, I went in and applied for it, too. In the end, I was the one who got the job.

The funny thing about haters is that they spend a lot of precious energy trying to make others miserable, but in the end, they hurt themselves most. The next time you run into someone who seems like he or she is out to get you, take a good, hard look at that person and then go look in the mirror. Chances are that the hater sees something in you that he or she wants, something that maybe you haven't yet seen in yourself.

Naysayers

A naysayer is different from a hater. While a hater is on a mission of destruction, a naysayer is someone who listens to an idea and says that it can't be done. A hater has no care for your well-being. He or she sees you as a threat and is out to crush you, whatever the cost. A naysayer, on the other hand, can be someone who loves you but holds you back from your full potential. A naysayer may lack understanding, be afraid for you, or think that your ideas are too big or too risky.

For example, as supportive as my parents were, I don't think that they really understood my vision. In my mind, I knew where I wanted to go and the steps I needed to take to get there. Of course, not everything pans out according to how we plan it.

My dad, in particular, often said those dreaded words: "When are you going to get a real job?"

My car broke down, and he said, "You need to get a car. There are a lot of things you need to do besides hanging around that radio station."

I understood what he was saying, and I knew that he wanted what he thought was best for me, but I wanted my dream so much that it gave me the push and drive to do everything it would take to get it. All the same, it was a struggle.

Maybe you've experienced the same thing in your life. Just remember that the world is full of haters and naysayers, but all it takes is one person who actually believes in you and gives you that shot to put you where you need to be. That person is out there, even if you haven't met him or her yet. Don't give up on your dream.

Exceed Expectations

When people say negative things to us, we tend to

internalize them. Then we second-guess what we're doing, and it feels like it's taking too long to reach our goals. We think to ourselves, "Man, maybe the haters and naysayers were right."

I interviewed 50 Cent back when he was on the rise in the industry but not yet as big as he is now. In that interview, I was open and honest with him about the way I perceived him, and I mentioned some of the things I'd heard about him from other people. He had his share of haters and naysayers.

I told him, "I really didn't want to interview you. I've heard so many negative things about you."

He responded, "You know, that's cool."

He wasn't fazed by the haters and the naysayers. His confidence and openness led to a great conversation. He told me something that stuck with me. He said, "I'm in a good space right now because I exceed the expectations of those around me."

He has a song, "In Da Club," that's about the celebration of life, but it makes mention of haters:[6]

> And you should love it, way more than you hate it. Oh you mad? I thought that you'd be happy I made it. I'm that cat by the bar toasting to the good life. Moved out of the hood. You trying to pull me back, right?

Then it goes on to say, "Go ahead and switch the style up, and if they hate, then let them hate and watch the money pile up!"

50 Cent and I have the same attitude: keep doing what you're doing despite the haters, and you'll be successful.

When I hear that song now, it reminds me that I have something of value I can offer the world, even when people don't see it. People tend to think that things are supposed to look a certain way. If you switch the style up and stay true to who you were born to be, it could mean going against set expectations, and that's never easy.

Be confident in what you have to offer. You were born with those gifts of yours on purpose. Stir up the change that is necessary, regardless of what others may say or think about you. Go out there and exceed their expectations. You may even exceed yours.

They Don't Get the Final Word

When it comes to your confidence and your motivation, look to the people who have your back, the ones who hold you accountable and speak the truth—even when it's a hard truth to hear—because they love you. You need to lean on those people when it feels like you aren't moving forward or when things are falling apart.

If you recognize haters in your life, take what they're saying with a grain of salt. It's okay to evaluate their words to see if there's any truth in them that you can use to grow, but remember that negativity is a force that impacts people in a bad way. If you allow haters' words to become part of your mental voice, you will severely hamper yourself in your efforts to build your dream.

At one of my radio jobs, I had to check the voicemail messages the listeners would leave for me. Every night, there was a message from a guy who would call in, cursing and criticizing me. It drove me nuts. There were times

I wanted to retaliate. I always wondered why he did that and why he didn't just change the station if I bothered him so much.

His calls really started eating at me. Then I changed the pattern of my thoughts. I probably had millions of listeners who enjoyed hearing me on the station. Just because they weren't calling in and heaping on the praise didn't mean they weren't there. Changing my perspective on the situation allowed me to move my thoughts away from that one negative caller. I focused on all of the positive things and was able to move forward.

When faced with haters, you need to consider the source and remember that you have something of value to offer the world. If that weren't true, they wouldn't be hating on you. When faced with naysayers, remember that their hurtful words stem from their own fears and insecurities and are ultimately rooted in love. Instead of letting one negative person pull you down, remember that he or she does not outweigh the dozens, or even millions, of people you will impact for good.

When the haters and the naysayers try to amp up the negative in your life, learn what you can from them. Then crank up the positive and move forward with your dream.

WORKBOOK

Chapter Four Questions

Question: Describe a time when you were distracted or derailed in your purpose by a hater. Did you allow this person's opinion to control you? What eventually helped you to overcome the negativity and criticism?

_____

_____

_____

_____

_____

_____

_____

_____

_____

Question: Who in your life is or sometimes can be a naysayer? What do you think is motivating this person's negativity? When the naysayer is someone who is close to you and truly cares about you, how can you separate yourself from his or her critical attitude without cutting the person out of your life?

_____

_____

_____

_____

_____

_____

_____

_____

_____

Question: If you stay true to who you were born to be, it could mean going against other people's expectations, which isn't easy. In what ways are you a pioneer, going against expectations or the norm? Consider people from the past who were pioneers in their fields.

How did they endure haters and naysayers?

_____

_____

_____

_____

_____

_____

_____

_____

_____

_____

_____

Action: Write down some favorite inspirational quotes, affirming words from friends and family, and big-picture dreams you have. The next time you are discouraged by the negativity of a hater or a naysayer, go back to these positive words and reflect on them. Ask yourself if there is anything true in the criticism from which you can learn, then throw out the rest. How will you allow this negative criticism to motivate you toward exceeding others' expectations and toward greater confidence and purpose in who you are meant to be?

Chapter Four Notes

CHAPTER FIVE

Losing to Win

Do you remember the quote from earlier about the greatest source of potential and wealth being found in the graveyard?[7] The reason that's true is because we fear the word *failure*. If we can't do it right the first time, why do it at all? *Because sometimes failure is necessary for success.*

I have so many ideas I want to explore, and I don't know where to start half of the time. There are so many dreams in my head, at times it's hard to know what to focus on.

We live in a world that tells us the key to success is being able to multitask. Work your day job. Work your side hustle. Have your hobbies. You can do it all at once!

In my experience, I've learned that I can achieve things more successfully when I'm able to focus on a single goal rather than shuffling through multiple activities at once. When you are fully focused, you can sort through all the ideas running through your head and find the ones that are most worth your time and energy.

"But what's that got to do with failing?" you ask.

When you focus on one overarching dream, you can evaluate if other opportunities you encounter are in your best interest. Will they help you to reach your goal? If they won't, you can spare yourself a future headache by letting them go and moving on to your next opportunity.

Sometimes it takes a failure for you to discover what you're supposed to focus on in your life. For example, my first on-air position as a radio personality after college was like a dream come true. The dream materialized very quickly, even though some of the challenges that went along with the dream were painful. Once I got my foot in the door, I got on the air within a short period of time, but that came to a screeching halt not long after. It was probably about a year from the start to the demise of that job. At the end of it, my job was dissolved, and I was fired.

After that, I took a part-time position at the competing radio station, which later turned into a full-time contract with a bonus structure, benefits and all. I stayed at that station for about six years. At the end of that time, I made a decision to try something new.

That newness only lasted for about a year. Then I was scrambling to try to find something to do. I was in the middle of a negotiation with a radio station that wanted me to do their slow-jam show. I thought for sure I would fall right into that and not even skip a beat. However, that wasn't the case. They ended up hiring someone else because he was willing to work for less.

I spent a lot of time looking for answers to the "What now?" question. I called one of my former bosses, and he told me, "Whoever hires you, get yourself back on the radio. People love you! I don't care how much money they're paying. You just need to be heard again, and the rest will fall into place."

I ended up taking a part-time position on the air. The job didn't pay me a lot of money, but as my father said, "A little dust is better than zero."

I was trying to make my mark in the radio industry, and while I had made some huge strides, I kept encountering setbacks. I felt like a failure, so much so that I couldn't move forward in anything. I had no idea how I was supposed to take care of my family. I spent a good many nights sitting in my basement, crying. Sometimes I would look out the window on a sunny day and cry because I was confused about what I was supposed to be doing with my life. At that point, things looked bleak. I felt like there was no hope for me to reach my goals.

But the loss I felt turned my focus to my true desires. If I had to do something, why not do something I was passionate about? Voice-over work was always something I wanted to do, but I didn't know how to get started.

I spent a lot of time on Google, trying to find some voice-over classes or workshops that would help me to enhance what I was already doing in that world. It seemed as if I couldn't find anything.

One night, I did a Google search, and I found a guy named Ed Green. Ed was one of the top voice-over guys in the industry, with a very extensive client list that included the likes of Paramount Pictures, Miramax, CNN, CNBC, Comedy Central, and 20th Century Fox.

Ed had an audition on his website for a potential voice-over artist to read on a phone line, so I decided to give it a shot. The next day, I unexpectedly received a call from Ed. We had a conversation that lasted almost an hour, and he gave me pointers on my delivery. He told me that I held my breath when I talked and that I did not properly use my teeth and tongue to pronounce words.

I was in awe of how much time he spent talking to me as a newcomer in the voice-over industry. He also told me that he believed I had the potential to be one of the greatest in the industry and that he'd be willing to drop his upcoming class to work with me one-on-one if I was interested. I gladly accepted. I began my one-on-one training with Ed, got my demos done, and started sending them out.

Losing my job and then settling for a part-time position felt like failure at the time, but it actually freed me up to pursue the work I truly wanted. If I'd had a full-time job, I wouldn't have been able to concentrate on working toward my dream. That shake-up allowed me to grow as an individual, and it changed my focus. It really forced me to unlock my true potential!

When I look back over the years, I see where I wasted a lot of time focusing on things that were secondary to my desired goals. Through those wasted opportunities, I learned that I must be proactive in order to reach my goals.

We have to be good stewards of the gifts and talents we're given and make the most of the time we have. Once time is gone, it's gone. You can never replenish that time. That's why it's important to start now and use the time you have available to do the things you desire and find purposeful.

It took losing a job that I was comfortable doing but

wasn't growing in and moving on to one that wasn't the greatest job in the world for me to learn what I needed to know. Feeling like I was spinning my wheels motivated me to pursue my real dream.

Pulling the Pieces Together

Are you in a similar place? Maybe you're feeling stuck in a dead-end job. Maybe your dream career ended up being a nightmare, and you don't know where to turn next. Maybe you know what you want to do next, but you lack the confidence to start.

Now is the time to start pulling the pieces together. The present is a gift. The future is not guaranteed at all. If you're in the middle of a tough season in life, start taking the necessary steps to correct your situation. Make time for the things you care about. When you have some down-time—I'm quite sure there's a moment in there somewhere—sit down and talk to yourself. Then listen. Sometimes you just need to be still so you can hear the voice of God. You already know some of your desires, and they can help to guide you to the true purpose of your life.

Look at Walt Disney and the failures that he saw in his lifetime. He didn't get to see all his dreams become a reality before he died. Disney World wasn't completed until 1971, and Walt Disney died in 1966, but he worked toward his goal during his life.[8] Today, that doesn't even matter. You see Walt's face, and you know exactly who he is. He is still such a brand name in this world that when you spot the iconic curly *D* on anything, you know that it means Disney.

Walt had a dream, and he inspired others to share his vision. To this day, people watch his movies, read his stories, and share in the magical worlds he created. People from all walks of life come to Disneyland or Disney World with one thing in mind, creating happy memories, all because one man dared to follow his dream. He faced numerous setbacks, such as the declaration of bankruptcy in 1923 and the resignation of many of the Disney animators in 1941,[9] but he continued the pursuit of his dreams.

When you face a failure, don't sit in a long-term pity party. Actively look for ways to change your situation. Ask yourself, "What's going to happen from here?"

Look back at where you came from and see what you can take away from those experiences. Look for how those things fit together because there is hope in every situation. There is hope in everything.

Failure: A Blessing in Disguise

Learning to look at failure as a blessing in disguise is very important as you work toward building your dream. When I look back on my life, I can connect all my jobs and see how they have brought me to the point where I am now. You may not always understand why you are in a certain situation when you're in the midst of a hard thing, but years later, after you've moved past it, you may be able to look back and see why you were there.

I remember standing on Hollywood Boulevard and talking to Jimmy Jam, one of the most sought-after producers in the music industry. He said, "Failure isn't always a bad thing, because it forces us to go."

Before becoming a producer, Jimmy and his partner, Terry Lewis, created a band in Minneapolis called Flyte Tyme. In those early days, they had a lead singer named Alexander O'Neal, and they toured all over Minneapolis. One day, they got a call from the great musical artist Prince. Prince told them that he wanted to take Flyte Tyme on tour with him, but Jimmy and Terry would have to get rid of Alexander. They replaced him with a guy named Morris Day and changed the name of the band to The Time.

Jimmy Jam told me that they knew Prince was going to call the shots. They knew that they weren't going to make a lot of money, but they were going to learn. He told me about their grueling rehearsals and about how Prince was so knowledgeable that they were able to learn from his experience and grow.

Jam and Lewis decided to take a break from the tour, and they went to Atlanta to produce a group called The S.O.S. Band. In the process of producing these records, they got snowed in and couldn't make it back to the tour they were doing with Prince. Prince fired both of them, but the record they produced for The S.O.S. Band ended up becoming a hit record, and it solidified them as producers in the industry.

Now they have a career that spans over three decades. They have a ton of number-one records and have worked with Janet Jackson, Michael Jackson, Aretha Franklin, Usher, Mariah Carey, Boyz II Men, and more.[10]

This amazing story illustrates that even when you lose, you can still win. They could have looked at being fired by Prince as the worst thing in the world. But they weren't on tour with Prince to make money. They were there to learn from a master, and they did. Then they took a risk that ultimately moved them into a successful career and opened up an entire new world of possibilities for them.

Trust the Process

Trust is a huge factor when it comes to overcoming a failure or setback. I'm a firm believer that our focus becomes our realization, our reality. If we change our focus, we can take those hard moments and trust that they're part of the process of building something successful.

Trust builds hope in our situation, and hope motivates us to pull ourselves out of what we are going through. Trust is a building block to get to the hope part of being successful. The trouble is that we tend to give up a little too soon and miss out on the victory that is within our grasp.

I was talking to a friend of mine about this very thing not too long ago. He asked me, "Have you ever seen that comic strip where these men are digging for gold? One of the men gets tired. He's like, 'Man, I give up.' And he walks away, but the other guy is still digging."

It was the second guy, the one who didn't quit, who got the gold that was just a little further down. The other guy gave up too soon.

You never know when your breakthrough will come. Trust the process. God placed that dream in your heart on purpose. Don't quit digging just because you feel like you're not getting anywhere. If you work hard and don't give up, you'll eventually reach your dream.

WORKBOOK

Chapter Five Questions

Question: Describe a failure you have encountered in pursuit of your passion. What did you learn from your failure? How did it change your focus and future path?

_____

_____

_____

_____

_____

_____

_____

_____

_____

_____

Question: What are some things on which you have wasted time because you were trying to do too many things at once instead of being focused and goal-driven? Are there projects you are currently undertaking that are distracting you from your real purpose?

_____

_____

_____

_____

_____

_____

_____

_____

_____

_____

Question: How can you trust the process when you are drowning in discouragement over failures or your dreams appear to be at a dead end? List three or more practical ways to keep up hope.

_____

_____

_____

_____

_____

_____

_____

_____

_____

_____

_____

_____

Action: Once time is gone, you can't replenish it. That's why it's important to start now and use the time you have to do the things you desire and find purposeful. Are you doing everything you can to use the time you have to work toward your dream? Make an action plan for the next week, month, and year. Outline important steps you want to take to make the most of your time and intentionally schedule your spare moments to work toward your goal.

Chapter Five Notes

_____

_____

_____

_____

_____

_____

_____

_____

_____

_____

_____

_____

_____

_____

_____

_____

_____

_____

_____

_____

_____

_____

_____

CHAPTER SIX

Loyal All the Way

Back when my wife and I first started talking, she would ask me about my five-year plan. My answers were all related to the station I was working for. I identified myself by that station at the time, and I couldn't see myself doing anything but that. Even when things got tough and I wasn't making the money I thought I deserved, I was willing to stick it out because I was loyal to them. After all, if I didn't have this job, what else would I do? It was a guaranteed paycheck every two weeks. Right?

Wrong! It took me years to understand that a guaranteed paycheck was far from the truth. At the end of the day, I was just an at-will employee. If you're unfamiliar with the term, *at-will employment* means that an employee can be dismissed (fired) for anything or nothing at all. Your boss doesn't have to provide a warning before terminating you, and if you are terminated, you can't file suit for wrongful or unjust termination.

Because of my sense of loyalty and because I believed

that loyalty would ultimately be rewarded, I had trouble letting go of my full-time job with XM Satellite Radio. It also felt more secure than doing voice-over work from home.

But sometimes security is an illusion. We've been trained to think that having a job with a company offers security. In truth, you're no more guaranteed long-term security working for someone else, including Fortune 500 companies, than you are working for yourself.

Maybe you're working for someone else because you know that it's a stepping stone on the path to your dream. If that's the case, do a great job for your own sake, even if you feel that you're being treated unfairly. If nothing else, it teaches you the value of having integrity, and it will better prepare you for the day you reach your dream.

Rise Above Mediocrity

Whether it's appreciated by your employer or not, loyalty is bound to catch the attention of others. When you were hired, your employer was taking a chance on you. You owe it to the job and to yourself to prove that you deserve the risk. That's why it's important to rise above the spirit of mediocrity and be the greatest employee you can be.

Mediocrity doesn't stand out, and you never know who's watching you, whether it's your direct supervisor or somebody outside of your company. You never know when somebody is getting ready to start something new and is looking for just the right person to fill a role. Or someone may hear of an opportunity you've been waiting for and know that you would be a great fit from seeing you in action. The person watching you may even be the person who ends up introducing you to the connections you'll need in order to turn your dream into a reality.

I recently had a chance to meet a guy named Joe Cipriano. Joe is a very successful voice-over artist whose story I've admired since first seeing him years ago on an *Entertainment Tonight* segment about voice-over artists. I've since read about him in a few publications. Joe and I discovered that we had worked in some of the same places and knew some of the same people, which shows just how small the world is.

You may not know Joe by name, but I'm certain that you've heard his voice on at least one of your favorite television programs. He has been the voice of *America's Got Talent, Hollywood Game Night, Deal or No Deal*, the Grammy Awards, and the Emmy Awards.

Joe, like myself, was a radio personality. He happened to be filling in on someone else's show when fate would have it that a FOX network executive was listening to the show. He thought that Joe would be a great promo voice for the network. The same guy who hired him as the voice for FOX TV was let go and landed another job at CBS. He then used Joe's talents as the voice for shows on CBS.

Now, just think if Joe had done a mediocre job when he was filling in, since it wasn't his show. Instead, his work ethic and integrity ended up turning into good fortune for him.

When you begin investing in yourself and holding yourself to a higher standard, you discover anew what your purpose in life is. You can be loyal to that purpose even while working at a job where you feel underappreciated. Love it or hate it, whatever you're doing today, give it your all. You never know who or what is waiting in the wings.

Integrity Matters

Who are you when no one else is watching? Your behavior, your practices, and your motivations behind the scenes define you as a person. Are you someone with integrity?

Your integrity matters. Even if you become an entrepreneur, you're still offering services to someone, and you still need to interact with people. You have to do a good job so they will keep hiring you and bringing you back. In fact, it's even more important to be someone with integrity if you're an entrepreneur since you don't have a "guaranteed" check every two weeks.

One of the most important things I've learned as an entrepreneur is that I really have to grind to get where I want to go. I have to establish relationships. I can't just sit back and wait for someone to hand me success. I go above and beyond for those who hire me because I am representing myself and the work I do. If I want to grow my business, I need to show my clients that I am reliable.

I'm not just sending them emails. I'm picking up the phone and calling them every now and again. I'm jumping on planes and going to see them. I want to make sure that everything is to their liking. It's more than a job to me. Integrity and loyalty mean going above and beyond in everything I do, and my dream thrives because of it.

Be Loyal to Your Dream

My career at XM Satellite Radio started because I jumped on something brand new. I didn't work directly for XM; I worked for a third party that provided content for XM. Unfortunately, the venture failed, and it was defunded within a year. Jobless, I called some of the people I was still in touch with from the job I left before starting at XM Radio, and I was told, "That's what you get for running and jumping on something."

I replied, "How can you say that? Nobody grows when they stay in the same place."

I pointed out to one of the guys I spoke with that he'd left a high-paying job to get where he was now. I'm quite sure that he was very comfortable financially, but he left that security to start his own communications company. He now owns his own radio stations.

You never know what's going to happen unless you take some risks. Sometimes you have to take a chance if you want to grow. Remember that if you aren't growing forward, you're growing stagnant.

I knew that XM Radio was a risk I wanted to take because it had the potential to get me that much closer to my dream job. I learned a lot from my time working there. I learned how to create my network. The woman who hired me challenged me to go through management contacts of artists and introduce myself in order to build up my industry network. I met more artists than I can count, and these people have actually become really good friends of mine.

The loyalty I had for my dream translated into loyalty in my work. I knew that everything I was doing was getting me one step closer to reaching my goal. It didn't matter that I wasn't there yet. I was taking steps in that direction. Even though certain aspects of the journey were less than ideal, I still invested loyally in them because I knew that they would help to get me where I wanted to go. Because of that loyalty, I felt connected to what I was doing, and I wanted to do a great job. Loyalty to my work got me to the place I am now and brought me a lot of opportunities along the way.

An opportunity presented itself for me to work directly for XM Satellite Radio after the third-party venture I'd worked with closed. While I was working in that new position, XM merged with Sirius. As I mentioned in a previous chapter, this merger was an uncertain time because many people lose their jobs when companies merge.

In fact, several of my friends lost their jobs during the merger. I was the only original XM on-air personality in the Hip Hop and R & B division who ended up keeping my job. Before the layoffs, a Sirius executive interviewed several of us and said, "When we have a merger of this caliber, there is no sense keeping two people to do the same job. I have sent my guys down here to try to weed out who we are going to keep."

He was straightforward with his purpose of being there, and I was straightforward with him, not allowing myself to be intimidated by his position of authority. I even told him that programming was not my desire. Although I was good at it, I enjoyed being on the air. I had no way of knowing what the outcome of my honesty would be, but I didn't think that I should lie just to keep a job, so I took a risk.

I found out later that I was initially put on a list to be let go. I don't know if it was the conversation with him that saved me, but I think that my loyalty and integrity played a part in my staying on. Years later, when I decided to step away from Sirius XM to concentrate on my entrepreneurship, I was asked, "You know, what if we took the other stuff away and just let you do your show?"

This was exactly what I wanted and what I'd articulated in that first meeting during the merger. I don't believe that I would ever have been offered this choice if I had just shown up and done only what I needed to do each day, nothing more. I chose to put everything into whatever I was doing in the hopes that the effort would allow me to reach my dreams.

It's easy to lose sight of our career vision because of the business culture in which we live. We think that success comes from climbing the corporate ladder, but I never wanted to do that. That wasn't in my DNA. I didn't want to be a manager. I didn't want to be a VP. I didn't want to be responsible for anyone else. That wasn't my desire. I just wanted to be on the radio, and I wanted to be compensated properly. Fortunately, I was able to achieve that, and it came from being loyal to my dream and to my job. If you want to reach your goals, you have to be loyal to your dream every step of the way.

Choose Your Loyalties Carefully

I read a book years ago called *Choosing to Cheat* by Andy Stanley.[11] The concept was so interesting: there are only twenty-four hours in a day and seven days in a week, so somebody has to get cheated somewhere. There's simply not enough time for everything we want to do.

For instance, I'm busy doing my radio show six days a week. In between, I do voice-overs for my recurring clients, audition for more work, and travel for work on occasion. All that alone is enough to fill an entire day. But what about my wife and my three kids? I can't neglect them.

The kids are involved in activities, my wife needs attention, and my wife and I need time together to keep that spark going in our relationship! How am I supposed to fit all of this into a mere twenty-four hours and still have time to rest?

It all comes down to sacrifice and prioritizing. I try to go to bed at a decent hour so I can get up by 3:30 a.m. to start my day. I start with preparation for my radio show by reading articles, watching the news, and taking notes. Some days, when I have voice work that comes in overnight, I will spend my early-morning window doing that work as well. At 5:30, I leave my studio and head upstairs to finish the kids' lunches for school, prepare breakfast for the family, and chat together before we all head our separate ways.

Once everyone is off to school, I head to the gym for about an hour and run a few errands if necessary. Once I get back, I pre-prep dinner if there's time and work in my studio, doing voice work as it trickles in. Then I start my radio show at noon.

As the kids begin to return from school, I make sure that they start their homework. Once I sign off of the air for the day, it's back in the kitchen to finish cooking dinner. Then we sit down to eat together as a family.

My wife and I have our window of time just to sit and talk about the day while the kids have their free time. Then it's time to rest up before I start the cycle all over again!

While it may seem like I have this time-management thing down to a science, there still needs to be some flexibility. There are times when I stay up all night because a creative force hits me, but I still make sure that I'm in the kitchen by 5:30 in the morning.

There are other times when I have to travel to visit clients, audition, or do a voice session outside of my studio. In those instances, my wife picks up the slack, or our great support system of parents and siblings helps us out. Then there are days when I have to take a break from it all and just relax so I don't burn out, and we take a trip somewhere as a family.

Even when I take time off from the radio, I still have to carve out part of the day for my voice work. Wherever I go, I take my portable set-up with me and inform my clients ahead of time that I will have a limited time window and won't be able to turn things around as quickly as I normally would.

Bottom line, as you work toward your dream, it's necessary to rearrange, take breaks, and sacrifice for those who love and care about you. Life isn't all about work and how much we can gain.

To what and whom are you going to be loyal? You have the same twenty-four hours in a day that I do. You have to choose your priorities wisely to make the most of your time. If you want to succeed in life, it's important to be loyal to your goals.

It's Up to You

Loyalty also matters when it comes to getting your hands dirty. Too often, people feel entitled. They want their dreams handed to them on a silver platter, and they don't want to put in the effort to grow. If you want to achieve your dream, you have to put in the work. Success doesn't come easily. There are a lot of bumps and bruises along the way.

Doors will be closed, and you will face a lot of rejection from a lot of people. That's why it's important to get rid of a sense of entitlement right out of the gate. Nobody owes you anything.

We can work together, and we can help each other to grow, but nobody is going to pave the road for you. *You* have to do the work to reach your goals. You were given a dream for a purpose, but it's up to you to pursue it loyally, wherever it leads.

WORKBOOK

Chapter Six Questions

Question: It's important to rise above the spirit of mediocrity and be the greatest employee you can be. Do you give your best, go the extra mile, and work with integrity? What about when you are working in a job that is less than your ideal? How can you rise above mediocrity and give your very best?

_____

_____

_____

_____

_____

_____

_____

_____

_____

Question: Sometimes you have to take a chance if you want to grow. A risk may be something as simple as being honest about your goals and skills instead of saying what you think a potential employer wants to hear. What are some chances you have taken that worked out for greater growth in your career? What are some risks you may need to take right now or in the future?

_____

_____

_____

_____

_____

_____

_____

_____

_____

_____

Question: Are you unconditionally loyal to your dream? How can this loyalty affect and enhance your current work situation? In what ways does your current job or position in life have potential to open doors for your future goals? How can you best utilize your current situation and leverage it for your dream?

_____

_____

_____

_____

_____

_____

_____

_____

_____

_____

Action: Who comes to mind when you hear the word *integrity*? Set aside time to talk to that person (or to read about the person if you don't know him or her personally) and to learn his or her secrets for acting with integrity even in difficult or seemingly dead-end situations.

Chapter Six Notes

CHAPTER SEVEN

What Is Success?

I think that the way we, as a culture, tend to define *success* isn't completely accurate. For many, a successful person is someone who has a lot of money in the bank or who has reached the top of his or her field. Furthermore, many people equate success and happiness as if it were the money or title itself that brings success and happiness to one's life.

I think that we all, to a certain degree, think about money as being a means to an end. It seems like people with a lot of money are happy and have no limitations to getting what they want. We all desire material things.

I used to define success by how much money I had. When I was younger, my goals and desires were driven from a material point of view, like owning a fine car and a big, fancy house. I wanted to make as much money as I could, which is one of the reasons I chose to get into the music industry.

As I grew older and experienced more of life, my

perspective changed. I didn't want to climb the corporate ladder or have countless zeros on the end of my pay stub. As I mentioned in a previous chapter, I just wanted to be the best me on the radio, and I wanted to be compensated appropriately for my skills and my work ethic. I also wanted to be the best husband and father I could possibly be. Achieving those three things became my definition of success, and the money became a bonus.

Another thing I've realized is that no matter how much money you make, there's still a sense of normalcy for every income level. I've come to realize that after buying a fancy car, it becomes just a nice car after about three months. The same can be said for just about anything that comes with a huge price tag. After a while, you get used to it.

I'm not saying that to discourage anyone from buying nice things. I think that actually adds a little spice to life. My point is that material possessions shouldn't be used to measure success. When it comes to success, happiness is the bottom line. You can be the most successful person in your field, but if you have no joy in what you're doing, what is the cost of your success?

A Better Way to View Success

I remember reading an article in *Entrepreneur* magazine that broke down what different billionaires and millionaires said about success, and none of them actually mentioned money.[12] Richard Branson, who is worth $5 billion, said that too many people measure how successful they are by how much money they make or by the people they associate with. In his opinion, true success should be measured by how happy a person is. It's the same idea I have. How does this person who owns his own private islands, who is about to launch a line of cruise ships, and who owns airplanes, record stores, and record labels define success? "It's just about being happy."

Mark Cuban, who owns sports teams, was also interviewed about the definition of success.[13] He said that success is waking up in the morning with a smile on your face, knowing that it's going to be a great day. He is now a billionaire, but he was happy and felt successful even when he was poor, living in an apartment with six guys and sleeping on the floor.

On the flip side, I've also noticed a lot of rich people who still have a void in their lives. They desire so much more than what they have. That sense of lack drives them to look for the next thing and the next thing after that to fill the void. I think that part of the feeling of lack comes from defining success as having a lot of money or material goods. They're trying to fill their lives with more *stuff*, but that's not what will make them happy.

You can have everything, but if you aren't happy, if you aren't doing the thing that lights you up every day, then you aren't successful. A wealthy friend of mine says that being rich only gives you more options; it doesn't provide happiness for you. In other words, if you think that *successful* means having the right number of zeros at the end of your checking account balance, you may be depriving yourself of happiness and sabotaging your own success.

You should measure success by the goals you obtain.

If you have a job with good hours, and that's what you desire, then you are successful. If you get a promotion or a job you've been dreaming about, then you are successful. If you set out to be the best husband or the best wife you can be, and you are, then you are successful. If you're actively working toward your goal of entrepreneurship, and that's what makes you happy, then you may not be the richest person in the world, but you are successful in a way most people only ever dream about.

Readjust and Redefine Your Priorities

I'm grateful that I found my passion at an early age. I fell in love with my career path and knew exactly what I wanted to pursue in life when most kids were applying for their first job working fast food. Being fifteen years old and getting a job at a radio station was amazing because I loved music. Falling in love with the job was something that came naturally because it nurtured the gift God had placed inside of me.

Getting to a place where I could support my family using that gift, that was work. But sticking it out, thanks to the support of certain people in my life, and watching it grow in directions I hadn't imagined as a fifteen-year-old boy, that's success.

People often struggle to find their path to success and what makes them happy. Take relationships, for example. Many people flip from one relationship to the next like songs on a playlist until they find "the one." Or they hop from job to job before they find the one they really desire. There are people who don't know what they want to do in life, and they feel so overwhelmed with the not knowing that they end up staying somewhere miserable because something is better than nothing.

Usually when there's a strong desire in you to do something, that's the thing that will make you happy. That's what you need to focus your attention on. Utilize your resources, such as books, the internet, and people who are doing the very thing you desire. It's like the Bible verse that tells us, "Faith without works is dead."[14] You have to put some action behind your goals and desires. Things don't happen by themselves.

Sometimes it takes years to develop a clear idea of what success looks like. Don't be surprised if, as you work toward building your dream, your definition of success changes along the way.

Who in Your Life Is Successful?

Take a look around you. Who would you say are the successful people in your life?

For me, it's my parents. There are a lot of things I didn't know about my mom until I was older. I knew that her parents were divorced, but I didn't realize what her father was like. I still remember the day I found out all she had been through in her childhood. We were at a workshop at church, and she opened up and shared about how abusive her dad was and how he would fight with her mother. I had no idea my mom experienced so much pain in her life. It broke my heart. I was literally sitting there crying as she shared.

My mother could easily have held on to the adversities

of her childhood and created a generational curse by passing on the same behavior to her children. But I never saw any indication of her childhood trauma in the way she raised my siblings and me. I never knew about the pain of her past until she decided to share that day.

I have always defined the measure of a woman by who my mother is. She always gives of her time and her resources. She taught school for forty years and didn't get paid a lot of money. Her passion for her work made teaching worth it to her, despite the smaller paycheck that came with it. She may not have the most prestigious career by some standards, but I look at her as a success story because she gives to others and *loves doing it.* It makes her happy to be able to serve, and that's what success is to me. She was able to achieve success coming from an upbringing that so many others are never able to move beyond.

Then there's my dad, my other role model for success. One day, he sat me down because I wasn't doing well in school, and I was ignoring everything my parents were telling me about the importance of my education. He told me the story of how he had to drop out of school after the seventh grade and take care of himself. I never knew that he went into the Job Corps in order to get his vocational training. As a child, I didn't notice him going to night school to get his high school diploma. My dad was a hard worker and rose to chief engineer at the National Institutes of Health with no college degree.

When I look at my dad, I see a natural-born leader. He has been a pastor for over twenty-five years. He's constantly looking for ways to expand his education by continuing to take classes and by attending seminars and conferences. He never gives up and keeps pursuing more to better himself and to be a blessing to others. When I look at him, I see a successful man.

Both of my parents are big success stories to me. They are happy individuals who live full lives and enrich the lives of others. Now I am in a space where I've reached some of the goals I made for myself when I was younger. I wanted to be on the radio, and I wanted to be a voice-over artist. I didn't know how I was going to do it, but I did it. I also wanted a good life for my family. My wife and I have worked hard to provide that for our children. When my kids look back over their lives, I want them to be able to see what it truly means to be successful and happy because of the examples that have been lived out right in front of them.

Look at the people in your life whom you consider successful. This can shed light on how you view and define success. It will also give you insight into what your priorities are or should be. Get to know the successful people around you and learn from them.

A Matter of Perspective

History is filled with examples of people who show us that the ideal we have of success is not necessarily what people experience in their lives. Even those who seem to have it all may be struggling just as much as you or I.

We can't define someone's success by his or her external circumstances because, at the end of the day, success is an internal perspective. Let's take my friend India Arie, who has sold over 10 million albums worldwide, has earned twenty-one Grammy nominations, and has won four Grammys. You would think that these accomplishments would make her very happy, but they haven't.

She and I have shared some pretty deep conversations, and she has been very honest about her battle with her self-worth. She told me that she feels like she is always recovering from some sort of battle. You'd probably think that someone who has written such beautiful and uplifting music would never feel this way. She also shared with me that there was a point in time when she didn't want to do music anymore.

As I think about some of the things she has shared with me, her song called "There's Hope" comes to mind. The song says:[15]

> Back when I had a little, I thought that I needed a lot. A little was overrated. But a lot was a little too complicated. You see, zero didn't satisfy me. A million didn't make me happy. That's when I learned the lesson. That it's all about your perceptions. Hey, are you a pauper or a superstar? So you act, so you feel, so you are. It ain't about the size of your car. It's about the size of the faith in your heart.

Then there's my friend Lalah Hathaway, who happens to be the daughter of one of the greatest soul singers, Donnie Hathaway. She can sing, and I've always viewed her as a successful person. I used to hear a lot of people say that she was underrated. One day while interviewing her, I asked, "How do you feel about your successes? I hear people talk about how underrated you are."

She responded, "I'm not underrated. I don't feel like

I'm underrated at all. Would I like to have more money? Sure, I would. Would I like to have a bigger house? Yeah. But I'm highly rated among those who have the opportunity or even take the time to rate me."

Sometimes success is a matter of perspective. You are the only one who can define if you are successful. No one else can label your life as successful or unsuccessful. Success isn't measured in monetary gain or definable accomplishments. Success is how *you* see your life.

I think that Maya Angelou said it best: "Success is liking yourself, liking what you do, and liking how you do it."[16] You may not live up to the expectations of others, and your life may not appear successful to others, but as long as you are happy with yourself and the work you're doing, you are successful, regardless of the material payout.

WORKBOOK

Chapter Seven Questions

Question: How do you see the relationship between success and money? Can you think of someone you consider
successful who is not materially wealthy? Why and in
what way is he or she successful? What can you learn
from this example of success?

_____

_____

_____

_____

_____

_____

_____

_____

Question: As you look back over your life, what do you see as your great successes? When are the times you were the happiest and the most satisfied? How has your view of success changed as you have grown and matured?

_____

_____

_____

_____

_____

_____

_____

_____

_____

_____

_____

Question: What character qualities make a person truly successful? How are you actively developing those attributes in yourself?

_____

_____

_____

_____

_____

_____

_____

_____

_____

_____

_____

_____

Action: Based on all of the above, write out your personal working definition of success. Put it up where you can see it often and keep your focus on what matters most to you.

Chapter Seven Notes

_____

_____

_____

_____

_____

_____

_____

_____

_____

_____

_____

_____

_____

_____

_____

_____

_____

_____

_____

_____

_____

CHAPTER EIGHT

Living It Forward

There have been many instances in my life when I felt like I had arrived. I felt like I had truly arrived in 1994 when I met my goal of being on the radio and went on the air as a radio personality. But looking back now, I would say, "That kid sounds like a mess."

That's the thing about life. If you're living it forward, you're always improving. Living it forward means that when you look back to revisit some of your past "arrivals," you can see that just as you needed to do some growing back then, you still have some growing to do now.

It's important to savor those moments when we feel like we've arrived, but we can't afford to get too comfortable there. I think the truth is that we don't ever actually arrive. Getting to be the voice of BET for a while was a huge accomplishment for me, but it became another comfort zone. At first, I was making a significant amount of money. My phone was ringing all the time. I did work for

TV Land and Cartoon Network. I even did some voice work for a top-selling video game.

Then, after a while, the phone rang less and less. I had to pick up the phone and start reaching out, making calls, and digging for more opportunities. Once that wealth of work dried up, I realized that I hadn't arrived at all.

The Cycle of Success and the Nature of Growth

That's the nature of external success. It comes and goes, which is why you always have to keep growing. Knowing this really helps me to stay focused. It causes me to keep my eyes open for new opportunities, and it keeps me learning.

I read. I take classes from other voice-over artists. I may not agree with everything they say, but it's still important for me to learn. As a result, I've picked up some concepts that I would never have thought about on my own. I can now apply these things to my voice-over career, and I'm able to use some of these new techniques in my auditions for other projects.

No matter what your career is, you can learn something from somebody else. Whether you agree completely with the other person or not, it's important for you to keep an open mind.

It's also important that you continue to dream. There are a lot of things I still desire to do. I want to do a television show someday. I've already shot the pilot for it, but as of this writing, it hasn't taken off yet. And that's okay because it allows me to surround myself with people who can use their talents to help me grow. Being able to focus on growth has led me into a variety of life and work scenarios, and many of these experiences are stepping stones to opportunities I might never have considered in the past.

A classic example comes from a conversation I had with Kenneth "Babyface" Edmonds. He has definitely been a success when one looks at his accolades, including writing and producing over twenty-six hit records for artists such as Boyz II Men, Whitney Houston, Bobby Brown, Madonna, and Toni Braxton. He has won eleven Grammys, has produced films and television shows, and has been honored with a star on the Hollywood Walk of Fame. There's even a twenty-five-mile stretch of Highway 65 that runs through his hometown of Indianapolis, Indiana, that is named after him.

On top of all that, Babyface has managed to have a career as a solo artist after performing with some successful groups via Manchild and The Deele. To have produced so many hits with so many great artists as well as in his own solo career, he obviously has a winning formula.

I found it to be rather interesting that a lot of the songs we have come to know and love were written long before they were ever placed with any artist. For example, the song "Roni," which was a huge hit for Bobby Brown, was written in 1982, and it came out in 1989.[17] There was the song "I'm Ready," performed by Tevin Campbell, that was written when Babyface was in high school. That just shows you that you never really know when your breakthroughs are coming.

I learned some valuable lessons during a conversation with Babyface. He told me that when things shift, we all can still afford to learn from others. For his 2001 album called *Face 2 Face*, he actually worked with some other producers outside of himself for the first time. He said that it was a little strange taking direction from some of the younger producers when he was used to being on the other side, doing the same thing they were doing, but he was willing to learn another way.

I believe that we can apply this to any industry because change is a part of everything and we all can continue to learn, which encourages our growth. Our ideas don't really change much unless we open up to others and apply some of the things we learn.

My friend Noel Gourdin is another good example of the cycle of success. Back when Noel released "The River," there was a record rep who was pushing his music in the direction of mainstream radio. I asked the rep for a copy of the CD, even though he told us that our listeners weren't the market he had in mind.

I thought that the song was incredible. I played it every day and shared it with other people, and everyone said that the song was amazing. I passed it along to my boss and said, "I think we should play this song on the radio."

We ended up putting it into the rotation, and when I saw that record rep the next week, I told him that we were playing the song. The rep's response was that they weren't even trying to market Noel's song anymore. I found out later that Noel was dropped from the label.

Still, we played that song for over a year, and the feedback was incredible. Steve Harvey heard us play it on our station and tried to figure out who the artist was. When he finally heard me say, "Noel Gourdin," Steve reached out to Noel and brought him onto his show.

Things started to take off for Noel Gourdin, and he became a huge success with a number-one record. Unfortunately, the music video didn't fit the concept of what his song was about, and his success took a backward turn.

That quick rise and fall hit him hard. As most of us would in his situation, he fell into depression. I still talk to him every now and again, just to check in, because I think that we have a responsibility to help one another. We all need the reminder that God doesn't bless us with a gift just for us to keep it for ourselves.

Noel recently called me and said that he is back on solid ground. He is doing music again, and he is doing well. He is in a different space now. He didn't take those times in his life that went dark and say, "There is nothing else I can do with this." Instead, he continues to push, and he's actively looking for ways to grow and evolve and to pursue his dream.

The will to press on and to grow is, in itself, a success. You may never make it "big time," but it's important for you to keep going and not stagnate, even when the circumstances in your life don't look like the success you originally envisioned. You have a gift you are supposed to share with the world, so don't quit when the road is bumpy. Press on and choose to turn every setback into forward motion.

We all go through growth processes of backward and forward, when it feels like we take one step forward and three steps back. But when we come out on the other side, we can point to these moments and say, "Even this led me down the road to success."

The Danger of Stagnation

When you put flowers in a vase, that water doesn't have anywhere to move around; it just sits there. When you throw the flowers away, the water stinks. What do you do with that water? You can't drink it, and you can't put anything else in it. It's no good for anything. You just throw it out.

That's exactly what happens when we choose not to grow. We just sit around and tell ourselves that this is all there is and all there ever will be. We feel like we've run out of anything worthwhile to offer the world, and we can't see any new opportunities in front of us. We get stuck because we aren't willing to change.

Essentially, stagnation is like being dead, like wasting away. You can be physically alive but mentally dead if you choose to stagnate. That's why it's important to take advantage of the time God has blessed you with and use it to the maximum. Stagnation is a choice. You are choosing to stay where it's familiar and comfortable, even when the water starts to stink.

When I was younger, I watched people move around and take positions in other places around the country just to stay in radio. They would work hard and ultimately be let go from jobs, even when they were in a top position, yet they were so passionate about radio that they would jump back in and go through the entire cycle all over again.

After seeing that happen, I decided that I needed to do other things in addition to my radio work, just in case. When I started working with BET, it was for one reason:

radio. But in meeting and networking with people, I was able to start a voice-over career because they requested that I do voice-over work. That created another opportunity for me to explore. By making myself available for something outside of my comfort zone, I learned to dream bigger and reach further than I'd dared to do before.

I often ask myself what my life would look like if I never made changes in order to pursue my gift and my passion. What if I were never courageous enough to take that first step of going from thought to action? For one, I wouldn't have the number of clients I have now because I wouldn't be focused primarily on voice-over work. I would be focused on what I was doing at whatever job I had, and I'd probably be frustrated and overwhelmed. I'd be spread too thin, doing too many tasks that didn't serve my purpose.

Change is necessary for growth, and change is always happening, whether we want it to or not. Even the most successful people have to deal with uncomfortable situations. They still have fears and doubts. But you don't grow when you stay right where you are the most comfortable. You fall behind. You stagnate. You don't unlock your potential.

It takes work to grow and to avoid stagnation, and sometimes it requires making big changes. You have to be vigilant and intentional, always stirring the water. You can't be so content in your comfort zone that you lose sight of the changes happening all around you. You have to change, too. Don't be afraid of change because without change, there's only stagnation.

Overcoming Burnout

One of the hard things we face when pursuing our dreams is burnout. Believe it or not, some of the biggest cases of burnout come on the heels of success. This is why it's important to surround yourself with people who can really support you.

There is a story in the Bible that I relate to about a man named Moses. Moses was the guy God invited to lead His people, the Jews, out of slavery in Egypt (Exodus 3). Talk about a big dream! At first, Moses made all kinds of excuses to avoid doing what God wanted him to do. However, later on, he took on so much of the responsibility that he risked burning himself out and leaving the people of Israel in a dangerous position.

God used the people in his life to give him some new perspective. His father-in-law, Jethro, took a look at all the things Moses was doing and suggested a new way of delegating tasks so that he wouldn't have to carry the burden of leadership on his own (Exodus 18). That advice didn't just benefit Moses; it allowed others an opportunity to step into the roles God had created for them to fill.

I, too, have built an incredible team along the way. My manager and business partner, Bobby Shields, is someone I've known all my life. We missed just about all of our teenage years and reconnected as adults. I would hear about all of the incredible things he was doing, like working with the Chris Rock Show and Dave Chappelle, and he would hear about things I was doing. We reconnected on a phone conversation and then met up in person.

We recognized each other's strengths and weaknesses,

and from that, we have been able to work together to create some incredible opportunities in the movie world and on-stage hosting, as well as the beginnings of a television show.

Successful people realize that they aren't cut out for every single task. They know when they need help and where to delegate certain responsibilities. In my life, I never have to do a negotiation because I've got agents who can do that. I don't feel comfortable in that space, but I surround myself with people who thrive in those situations.

Take a look at your network. Do you see some strengths other people possess that may complement your weaknesses? Are there areas where they struggle but you excel? Perhaps they can be the right arm, and you can be the left. In this life, everybody has a role to play, and one role is not better than another.

Your network is like a group of family and friends. (Of course, some family members are closer to you than others.) These are the people you can lean on and who've got your back when things get tough. Maybe your business has grown to a point where you have to start re-evaluating some processes in order to take it to the next level. Or maybe you've hit a slump, and things aren't going as well as you'd hoped. Maybe you're wondering if you should walk away from a venture entirely. Having the outside perspective of your network will help you to continue moving forward when it feels like you're slipping backward.

There's Still Work to Be Done

Like I said before, I don't think that people ever really "arrive," even though they may gain success in the pursuit of their dreams. The world is always evolving, and things are constantly changing. The trend that's hot today is old news tomorrow. Even songs that top the charts for weeks eventually fall off the radar.

Our evolving world means that you have to continue growing personally and professionally. If you want to be successful, you have to keep evaluating what you're doing and why. Are you still working toward bettering the world for others, or have you reached a point where you're moving through your days on autopilot? Are you thriving, or are you merely surviving?

As you work toward building your dream, remember that there will be people in your life who can see the potential in you that you don't always see in yourself. When you find yourself stagnating or approaching burnout, sometimes it takes another person to ignite the spark that gets you motivated back into forward motion.

Pay attention when someone says, "I see you can do this" or "You should really pursue that." Take the time to evaluate what the person is saying. You may not be ready to take that leap yet, but when the time comes, it may open you up to a new array of possibilities. It may be exactly the thing you need to keep living it forward.

WORKBOOK

Chapter Eight Questions

Question: Describe a time when you achieved something you really wanted and felt like you had truly arrived. How is that past success different from your goals for today? How have you continued to dream and to set new goals for your success?

_____

_____

_____

_____

_____

_____

_____

_____

_____

Question: What are some of the reasons why great success might be followed by depression or a sense of failure? If you were to achieve your greatest dream today, what follow-up goals could you begin pursuing tomorrow?

_____

_____

_____

_____

_____

_____

_____

_____

_____

_____

_____

Question: Which is the greater struggle for you personally, stagnation or burnout? What steps can you take to keep learning and trying new things to avoid stagnation? What areas can you delegate or better prioritize to avoid burnout?

_____

_____

_____

_____

_____

_____

_____

_____

_____

_____

_____

_____

Action: Talk to people who are close to you and ask them for their observations. Where can they see you being successful? What new training or further education do they recommend that you pursue to enhance your current skill set? In what areas do they anticipate that you will be successful, or how can they visualize you building on your current success?

Chapter Eight Notes

_____

_____

_____

_____

_____

_____

_____

_____

_____

_____

_____

_____

_____

_____

_____

_____

_____

_____

_____

_____

_____

CHAPTER NINE

The Best You

I believe that each individual is created uniquely. People may try to emulate you or what you do, but they will never be as good at being you as you are. On the flip side, you can try to emulate someone you look up to and admire, but you'll never be as good at being that person as that person is. That person is unique and uniquely suited to his or her life path, just as you are uniquely suited to yours.

There was a point early on in my career when I tried to emulate the people from whom I was learning. It was helpful to a point, but as I got to know myself better and became more confident in who I was designed to be, I found my own lane, my own uniqueness, and I came up with my own creative ideas.

For example, when I do a celebrity interview, I don't even want to be in the same room as someone else who is interviewing the same person. I try not to talk about the upcoming interview because I want my conversations to be unique and organic. I don't want to pick up things from other people that will influence how I approach the situation, because I am my best when I'm being myself.

As you learn more about yourself and what works best for you, you'll be able to make self-improvements that will help you to build on your dream. This self-awareness is key to being successful.

The Importance of Self-Awareness

There are several different types of personality profiles out there that are helpful for determining how you'll respond to different situations and stressors. Some companies even have each new employee take a personality test during the hiring process so they can determine if that individual will be a good fit for the organization. They know that it's important to understand who their employees are and recognize their personality types.

For instance, I'm someone who works best when under pressure. It's something I learned about myself a long time ago. I'm a procrastinator by nature. I wait until the last minute to do everything. When I want to get into a creative space, it doesn't hit me immediately. I've learned to let my mind process things in the background. I could be sleeping when an idea hits me, and then I get up and get to work.

My wife is a planner and an organizer. If she wants to go out and run some errands, she will write out a list first. Sometimes she'll come into my studio and say, "Oh my gosh, I need to clean this place up." And I'll say, "No, leave stuff as is."

It seems like clutter to her, but I'm comfortable in my space. We also handle stressful situations differently. She may sweat the details that don't faze me. I don't get stressed out to the point that little things throw me off course.

It's important to know who we are and how we respond to situations because it will help us to know how to approach our goals. There's nothing certain about life, and its pieces are always moving. Learning how you handle the unexpected and unpleasant aspects of life is vital to being successful in pursuing your dreams. But knowing who you are isn't a one-time, overnight revelation.

Self-awareness comes from taking the time to discover who you are. You have to spend time with yourself and observe how you respond to different situations. It's something you develop over a period of time. It can come from life experiences and self-reflection, but it can also come from what other people say about you. The haters that I spoke about earlier can actually point out things about you that you might not have seen before. But you have to know yourself well enough to be able to take what they're saying and recognize what is true and what isn't. The same is true about feedback from your supporters. Ultimately, self-awareness comes from being able to examine yourself and be open-minded enough to receive feedback from others. Then you use that information to grow personally and professionally.

Move Beyond Fear

If you're going to pursue your dreams, you have to

learn to move beyond your fear. Accept that you may get bumped and scraped along the way, knowing that each hurdle and obstacle you face brings you one step closer to your desired goals. If you don't find a way to move beyond your fear, you're going to find yourself wondering what would have happened if only you had tried. That should be motivation in itself.

It takes faith, determination, and prayer to step fully into who you were born to be and pursue the dreams God placed inside your heart. If you're struggling to take that next step, try stepping away from the noise. Take the time to sit alone and meditate. Think about the things that are holding you back. Ask yourself how the decisions you make today will impact your life down the line.

If you still need a helping hand, seek guidance from the people whom you can genuinely trust to give you sound advice. This is where your cheerleaders come in handy!

When I set out on this venture and left my full-time job to focus on doing voice-overs, I didn't share it with a lot of people. I didn't want to hear all the negative comments from the people who either didn't share my vision or didn't have my best interests in mind. My wife was on my side, and she continually pushed me to move beyond my fear and step into my passion and calling in life. Having that support in place was crucial for me to take the bold steps when I wasn't sure where they would lead next. Reading motivational books and biographies about successful people also helped me to get past some of my fears.

It's hard to believe, but there are plenty of people who are as scared of success as they are of failure. I think that

I was one of those people early on. I got so used to hearing "no" all the time, even though I knew that I had potential, that I started worrying about what would happen if someone said "yes."

One day, before I took the big step of pursuing my dream full-time, I went to audition for a soap opera. I walked into the room, cracking jokes and just being myself. Then I read the script opposite the actress in the room. A woman who was there pulled me to the side and asked, "Have you ever taken any acting classes?"

I said, "No, I haven't."

"You should consider taking some acting classes because it will enhance what you already have naturally. If you move to L.A., I can almost guarantee someone will pick you up. Would you move?"

I said that I would. I was talking like I was brave, but when I got home and sat down, I thought, "No, I don't want to do that." I was scared to death about how such a risk would change my life. It would take me out of my comfort zone in every way imaginable, and I wasn't ready for it.

I think about all the things I could have done but was too scared to do at the time. Fortunately, I've discovered that as long as we're breathing and we have our health, it's not too late to jump into the thing we may be afraid of doing. Use what you have now to take that first step. Do what you can with it and watch how those skills and experiences multiply into other opportunities.

Ultimately, if you want to take the risks necessary to pursue your dreams, you have to know who you are and who you want to be. I'll say it one last time: God didn't plant a dream in your heart and give you a gift so you could hide it. Nobody can offer the same gifts to the world that you can. Once you accept that, you can open up, learn who you are, and put all your experiences together to get where you want to go.

My last piece of advice to you is to be open-minded during the process of self-discovery. It's the same advice I give myself. Look in the mirror and accept who you are because you are unique. You possess a great gift with your uniqueness. Spend some time with yourself and get to know who you are. It's only then that you'll be able to take the next step in becoming all you can be.

WORKBOOK

Chapter Nine Questions

Question: What is the difference between learning from someone's example and trying to be that person? How can you learn from others but still remain true to the person God made you to be?

_____

_____

_____

_____

_____

_____

_____

_____

_____

_____

Question: What fears are currently holding you back from pursuing your dreams? List anything that is getting in your way. Then seek ways to overcome each obstacle through your faith and your network of family and friends.

_____

_____

_____

_____

_____

_____

_____

_____

_____

_____

_____

Question: What unique gifts, perspectives, or dreams do you have to offer the world? What could be lost if you don't live up to your full potential to be the best you that you can be?

_____

_____

_____

_____

_____

_____

_____

_____

_____

_____

_____

_____

Action: Explore different personality types (for instance, the Myers-Briggs types) and discover which one or ones best characterize you. How do people with your personality typically work best? How do they respond under pressure, and how do they interact best with others?

Chapter Nine Notes

_____

_____

_____

_____

_____

_____

_____

_____

_____

_____

_____

_____

_____

_____

_____

_____

_____

_____

_____

_____

_____

CONCLUSION

Go Do Something!

If you were sitting in the chair across from me like the people I interview, I'd tell you to go out and pursue your dreams. Getting an education is a part of it. Knowing who you are is a part of it. Time is of the essence, but that doesn't necessarily mean that things will happen overnight. You'll get bumps and bruises, and there will be some failures along the way. It's all a part of your journey. Take those rough patches and celebrate them. They are steps to your success, and they'll help you to grow.

Never forget that there is a difference between going to a job every day just to meet your needs and staying true to the dream that was placed in your heart. If what you're doing brings you joy, that is what you should be doing. If not, take the time to evaluate what it is that you want out of this life you're living.

Go *do* something. It's not enough to have a dream if you put no action into making it a reality. Start throwing those ideas up against the wall. Not all of them are going to stick, but it just takes one.

Remember the lesson of the graveyard. All that unrealized potential. All those unfinished dreams. All those unlived futures. Don't let your dreams be buried with you.

Surround yourself with people who believe in you and cheer you on, people who tell you not to give up. I know that you already have at least one person cheering for you. I know because I am.

Just as my wife holds me accountable every day that she cheers for me, I am now holding you accountable. I'm holding you accountable to go out, to be successful, and to be happy.

You can do it!

About the Author

From volunteering at a radio station as a teen and enduring obstacles throughout his journey to success, Cayman Kelly now has over twenty years of on-air experience, including hosting his national show on Sirius XM Heart & Soul. Additionally, he has become an entrepreneur and voice-over artist who has been featured on television and in commercials, movies, video games, and more. Even more than his professional success, Cayman is proud to be a husband and a father of three and to have found a way to do the work he enjoys while being devoted to the family he loves.

REFERENCES

Notes

[1] Goins, Jeff. *Real Artists Don't Starve: Timeless Strategies for Thriving in the New Creative Age*. HarperCollins Leadership, 2017, p. 129.

[2] Tijani, Mayowa. "'The Wealthiest Place on Earth Is the Cemetery' and Other Memorable Myles Munroe Quotes." *The Cable*. November 10, 2014. https://www.thecable.ng/wealthiest-place-earth-cemetery-%E2%94%80-memorable-munroe-quotes.

[3] King, Martin Luther, Jr. Quoted in *Oxford Essential Quotations*. 5th ed. Edited by Susan Ratcliffe. Oxford University Press, 2017. https://www.oxfordreference.com/view/10.1093/acref/9780191843730.001.0001/q-oro-ed5-00006293.

[4] Reynolds, Kevin, dir. *187*. Icon Entertainment International, 1997.

[5] Whitworth, William. "Kentucky~Fried." *The New Yorker*.

February 6, 1970. https://www.newyorker.com/magazine/1970/02/14/kentucky-fried?subId1=xid:fr1576604088081aaj.

[6] Jackson, Curtis James, III. "In Da Club." *Get Rich or Die Tryin'*. Aftermath, 2003.

[7] Tijani, "The Wealthiest Place on Earth Is the Cemetery."

[8] "Walt Disney Biography." Biography.com. August 21, 2019. https://www.biography.com/business-figure/walt-disney.

[9] "Walt Disney Biography."

[10] Tannenbaum, Rob. "Producer Jimmy Jam Pays Tribute to 'Ultra Sharp, Ultra Witty' Prince: 'His Talent Was Singular, Second to Nobody.'" Billboard. April 26, 2016. https://www.billboard.com/articles/columns/pop/7348342/jimmy-jam-remembers-prince.

[11] Stanley, Andy. *Choosing to Cheat.* Doubleday Religious Publishing Group, 2003.

[12] Patel, Deep. "Richard Branson's 8 Keys to Happiness and Success." Entrepreneur. April 22, 2019. https://www.entrepreneur.com/article/331932.

[13] "Mark Cuban's Definition of Success." Steiner Sports. December 19, 2014. https://www.youtube.com/watch?v=mVK7ycmlV4A.

[14] "James 2:14–26." New King James Version. Thomas Nelson, 1982.

[15] Simpson, India Arie. "There's Hope." Track 6 on *Testimony: Vol. 1, Life & Relationship*. Universal Records, 2006.

[16] Angelou, Maya. Quoted in Amanda Macias, "15 Pieces of Advice from Maya Angelou." Business Insider. May 28, 2014. https://www.businessinsider.com/maya-angelou-quotes-2014-5.

[17] Kawashima, Dale. "Special Interview with Kenneth 'Babyface' Edmonds, Legendary Songwriter and Artist, and Songwriters Hall of Fame Inductee." Songwriter Universe.

March 20, 2017. https://www.songwriteruniverse.com/babyface-interview-2017.htm.